Original title:
Pocket Watches and Daydreams

Copyright © 2025 Creative Arts Management OÜ
All rights reserved.

Author: Dorian Ashford
ISBN HARDBACK: 978-1-80586-025-9
ISBN PAPERBACK: 978-1-80586-497-4

Journeys Beneath the Dial

Tiny hands go round and round,
Time travelers on a merry ground.
With every tick, a giggle flies,
Chasing dreams 'neath laughing skies.

A rabbit hops, a cat sings low,
As minutes dance, they steal the show.
Each chiming hour brings a jest,
In this land, time's quite a guest.

Crystals of Forgotten Hours

Through glassy gems, bright stories shine,
Once lost in clocks, now sipping wine.
They twirl and spin, while snoring cats,
Conjure jokes on their fancy hats.

A lizard clinks with dandy grace,
As sundials smile at a funny face.
Ticklish seconds squeeze our sides,
In a world where laughter rides.

Enchanted Moments

In a whirl of sparkles, a twinkling cheer,
Time comes alive, and tickles our ear.
A flick of the wrist, a giggle or two,
When fairies decide to pull a fast screw.

With each little blip, a hiccup appears,
As jumbled seconds dissolve our fears.
In winks and blinks, life starts to zoom,
Prancing through time in a vibrant room.

The Rhythm of Forgotten Wishes

A waltz of dreams beneath the stare,
Of aged old clocks caught unaware.
They stumble through requests not heard,
As wishes weave their quirky word.

With jests afloat on a breezy tide,
They tickle hearts where whims reside.
Time's silly dance draws laughter near,
In this space where whimsy steers.

Twilight Ticks

In twilight's glow, the hands conspire,
To dance and twirl, like a silly choir.
Time slips on banana peels,
Tick-tock laughter, how it feels!

A bird ticked off, sang off-key,
While time played hide and seek with thee.
Chasing shadows in a wobbly race,
Each tick like a joke in a silly place.

Dreams Held Close

Holding a thought as if it's gold,
Wishing on wishes, never too bold.
A giggle hides in each little gleam,
Time laughs back at a waking dream.

Cupcake thoughts and jellybean plans,
Running in circles, we hold hands.
A whimsical watch where minutes collide,
Tickling time with joy as our guide.

Reflections in a Silver Case

Peering in silver, I see a jest,
Time wearing funny hats, oh what a fest!
Bouncing mirrors with giggles galore,
Reflecting moments I can't ignore.

A silver shark swimming in a race,
With jellybeans popping all over the place.
Time wears mismatched socks, what a sight,
In a whirl of giggles, morning to night.

Timeless Treasures

We hoard our laughs in a rusty chest,
Each chuckle a gem, we're truly blessed.
Ticklish moments tucked away tight,
Shimmering brightly in playful delight.

Unruly time dances in the air,
Winking at us with a teasing flair.
Cherishing silly amidst the mundane,
Timeless treasures, oh, let's entertain!

Songs of the Silent Ticker

In a pocket, time takes a seat,
With gears that dance, they skip a beat.
Minutes prance like a hungry cat,
Tick tock, tick tock, where's the hat?

Jokes are whispered in candid glances,
As seconds slide through playful dances.
A watch that laughs and winks with glee,
Oh, what a thrill, the time's so free!

Labyrinths of Languid Time

In winding ways, we lose our place,
As tickers tease with a cheeky face.
Pacing here, there, lost in the fun,
Is it noon or still the morning sun?

The hands are spinning with silly pride,
As laughter echoes in every stride.
Where did the minutes run off to?
A maze of joy, just me and you!

Spirals of Nostalgia

Round and round like a circus show,
Memories burst like popcorn, whoa!
Tickling hearts with a playful twist,
What a delightful time can't be missed!

In every tick, a story spins,
Of past adventures and eager grins.
With snickers and chuckles, we reminisce,
Finding joy in time's sweet abyss.

The Artisan's Keep

In a workshop filled with crafty dreams,
Gears giggle as they burst at the seams.
Escapades of clocks with a wink so bright,
Chasing shadows until the night.

Crafted smiles from the artisan's art,
Making time twist, pulling at the heart.
Each tick a joke, each tock a tease,
Creating laughter like a gentle breeze.

Chasing Shadows of Yesterday

Tick-tock, I lost my shoe,
Running late, oh what to do!
Time flies by, it does a dance,
But here I am, still in a trance.

Chasing dreams that slip away,
Like sandcastles made of clay.
With every tick, I change my mind,
Oh what a riddle, to unwind!

The Midnight Hour's Embrace

As the clock strikes twelve, I grin,
The midnight snacks begin to spin.
With cookies dancing on the shelf,
  I join the party all by myself.

Time's a trickster, what a tease,
It winks at me with perfect ease.
I laugh aloud, a joyful cheer,
Who cares if sleep is nowhere near?

Glances at Infinity

Peeking through a glassy stare,
I catch a glimpse of wild hair.
Time's a jester, full of glee,
Each second's long, or so it seems.

Beyond tomorrow, what a ride,
With giggles tucked away inside.
For every tick and every tock,
I give a wink, just like a clock.

Memories of the Mechanical Heart

A whirring sound, so sweet and bright,
My heart's a clock, it beats at night.
With every gear and every spring,
It sings a song only I can bring.

Time's a friend, though a tricky chap,
I set the dial, then take a nap.
In dreams, I dance with all my foes,
Tickling time as it unfurls and flows.

Echoes of Lost Time

In a world where minutes smile,
Tick-tock dances through the aisle.
Gears chuckle in a vivid thrift,
Time's jesters play, a shimmering gift.

A watch whispered to a spoon,
"What's the rush? We'll be here soon!"
Chasing seconds on a flighty breeze,
While clocks conspire with the bumblebees.

Dreams Woven in Gold Chains

A chain of gold around my neck,
Holds dreams of snacks and time to wreck.
Sandwiches sing of lunchtime lifts,
And calendars tease with sweet little gifts.

Tickled thoughts drift in the air,
As watches giggle without a care.
A fumble here, a tumble there,
Time shows off with a playful flair.

The Clock's Lament

The clock did chime a quirky tune,
Wishing for a lazy afternoon.
Pendulum sways with a raucous laugh,
Counting metrics of a silly half.

Swept away in a whirl of time,
Its hands moonwalk in rhythm and rhyme.
Sitting on a shelf, proud as can be,
Tickling thoughts like a ticklish bee.

Chasing Shadows of Yesterday

Shadows strut in the fading light,
As laughter trails on a whimsical flight.
Previous moments in goofy arrays,
Bleed into today's merry misplays.

A misfit clock loses track of the sun,
Dancing along with a friend for fun.
Synchronizing giggles like children at play,
Chasing echoes that cheerfully sway.

Shimmering Seconds

In my pocket, a gleam, a twinkle,
Time dances like a winking sprinkle.
Tickling hours with a little tease,
Laughter bursts like gentle breeze.

Chasing minutes around the room,
A jester's game, a joyful zoom.
Time hops like a playful pup,
Twirling round in a cheeky sup.

With every tick, a secret joke,
Whispers of the time we broke.
Giggles echo in this crazy spree,
While seconds tumble, wild and free.

In the tick of a quirky dance,
We twirl through time in a silly trance.
Counting laughs rather than the clock,
For every tick is a playful rock.

Echoes of a Lost Minute

One minute gone, where could it go?
Perhaps it joined a silly show.
Clowns in hats with shoes too big,
Left the ticking clock to jig.

I searched for seconds on a spree,
Found a lost tick beneath a tree.
It chuckled softly, tapping its toes,
Playing hide and seek in funny clothes.

With each chime, I sneak a peek,
At the jesters of time, oh so unique.
They tumble and giggle behind the gears,
Wrapping me up in a web of cheers.

Never mind those minutes missed,
Laughter creates the perfect twist.
We chase the seconds, wild and fleet,
With echoes of joy that can't be beat.

Threads of Time

With threads of silver, time weaves on,
A tapestry where pranks are drawn.
Naughty needles in a playful bind,
Spinning laughter, what a find!

Each stitch a joke, a little wink,
Colors burst as clocks all blink.
Tickled threads in a jolly twist,
Knots of giggles we can't resist.

Fabrics of fun in every seam,
Woven moments that make us beam.
A fabric that shouts, "Let's do it again!"
Laughter stitches through joy and pain.

As time unfolds its silly guise,
We unravel moments that surprise.
Together we laugh through the weave and weft,
In a world where joy is always left.

Serene Tick-Tock

In a peaceful corner, the clock does chime,
With a serenade of sweet, silly rhymes.
Tick-tock whispers on comfy chairs,
Carrying giggles through the square.

A calm display of time in play,
Sending worries a mile away.
Each tick a smile, each tock a cheer,
In this cozy nook where fun is dear.

Time's parade walks on fuzzy toes,
Dancing gently as the laughter flows.
Caught in laughter's warm embrace,
We find joy in this gentle space.

So let the clock's soft tick-tock sing,
In harmony with the joy we bring.
A serene place where time delights,
With giggles echoing through the nights.

Ballads of a Clockwork Heart

In a world where gears do sing,
A heart of springs, the joys they bring.
Time waltzes with a playful grin,
Tick-tock laughter, let the fun begin.

A jester's cap upon a clock,
With every chime, a funny knock.
Dancing seconds, spinning fast,
In this realm, joys forever last.

A cuckoo pops, a dizzy show,
With every hour, the giggles grow.
Count the beats, they never fail,
As we ride on this laughter trail.

So hear the tune of whimsy's call,
In this merry land, we'll have a ball.
For every tick and every tock,
Unraveled fun around the clock.

Glimpses of Neverland

In a garden where the shadows play,
Butterflies giggle, then fly away.
A sly old fox with a timing trick,
Makes me chuckle with every lick.

Below the trees where dreams abide,
The sun and moon both take a ride.
With every glance, my heart does skip,
As we sink deep in a laughter trip.

A pirate ship made of candy bars,
Sailing swiftly among the stars.
Tickled by whispers from the breeze,
Here's a treasure, if you please!

In this land of pure delight,
Where giggles dance through day and night.
With every glimpse, a fleeting tease,
Oh, what fun and such sweet ease!

The Dance of Time

A waltz begins when clocks align,
With moons and suns, a wacky sign.
Step to the left, then twirl on right,
In this foxtrot, laughter's in sight.

The hours leap like froggy friends,
Taking turns where the fun never ends.
With a spin and dip, we glide so free,
Time has never been this silly!

Raindrops fall, a splishy-splash,
In this dance, we make a splash.
Tickled feet and gleeful squeals,
Our laughter swirls, our joy reveals.

In this frolic through the night,
Every glance ignites a light.
So jump into this merry rhyme,
And dance away with goofy time!

Beyond the Ticking Realm

Past the tick, beyond the tock,
There's a place where laughter rocks.
Time's a trickster with playful schemes,
Crafting joy from silly dreams.

In a river of hours, we sail so bright,
Oars of giggles, a comical sight.
The sun gives a wink and the moon, a grin,
As we chase after the fun within.

With each second, a new joke told,
The laughter fades, but never cold.
A whimsy path where playfulness gleams,
In the world of joy, we're kings and queens.

So let's journey far, my giggling friend,
To where moments of laughter never bend.
In this ticking realm, we'll always find,
The beats of fun that tickle the mind.

Reflections in a Dial

In the shop, they shine and gleam,
Ticking softly, a silent team.
Each face reflects a joke or two,
As time winks back, it laughs at you.

A watch with legs runs out the door,
Chasing time like never before.
With every tick, a giggle loud,
The gears conspire, they're feeling proud.

Round and round, they whirl away,
Counting laughs throughout the day.
A jester's bow, a clown's disguise,
Time's folly under bright blue skies.

So let's all wind up this charade,
And dance with time, our own parade.
For in each turn, a jest awaits,
Life's clock ticks on, but never waits.

Memories in Motion

A clock spins tales of when we fell,
With laughter ringing like a bell.
Tick-tock echoes of silly spins,
Remind us how the fun begins.

Mismatched hands, they twist and sway,
Stumbling through the light of day.
Hours bounce like kids at play,
All the while, the minutes stray.

Chasing seconds, a silly race,
Each tick brings joy, a silly face.
Time's a jester wearing charm,
In its grip, we come to harm.

Memories whirled in gears so bright,
Whirling smiles from morn to night.
So let's embrace this joyful spree,
And keep on laughing, wild and free.

The Hourglass of Fantasy

An hourglass with sand so quick,
Spills out jokes, a magic trick.
Each grain a laugh that flies away,
In our hearts, they love to play.

The sandman wears a silly grin,
Filling dreams that spin within.
Hours tick-tock, but don't be coy,
For every grain's a burst of joy.

Flip it over; it's time for fun,
Whirling laughter, we'll never run.
In this glass, let whimsy thrive,
As every joke keeps dreams alive.

So come and dance with every grain,
Let's laugh till we're both insane.
In this timeless art we find,
The sand sings sweet, our hearts unwind.

Enchanted Minutes Under the Stars

In midnight's glow, the stars take flight,
With minutes dancing, oh what a sight!
A twinkle winks with a silly cheer,
As laughter echoes far and near.

Time takes a break on this calm night,
While giggles float on pure delight.
Each second whispers tales so bright,
Under the moon, all feels just right.

Enchanted moons with playful beams,
Paint our thoughts like silly dreams.
Tickling time with cosmic glee,
In our hearts, wild jesters flee.

So join the jest with stars above,
And dance along with those we love.
For every moment brings a grin,
In the grand clock, we all spin.

Shadows of the Sundial

In the yard, the sun casts shapes,
A shadow dance, as time escapes.
Cats seem to plot their sunny naps,
While bees conspire in silly laps.

The flowers giggle, swayed by breeze,
Tickling each other with such ease.
A borrowed hour slips through the air,
As squirrels giggle without a care.

A bird lands clumsy on a fence,
Watches the world from his own tense.
He whistles tunes that make us grin,
As time forgets where it's been.

We chase the moments, full of glee,
With every tick a jubilee.
The sundial grins; it knows the score,
It's never late, it's just a bore.

Between the Gears

A clock was struck by funny fate,
The hands danced quick, they just won't wait.
One swung wide, the other just pouted,
While pendulums around us shouted.

The gears get tangled in a twist,
Each tick a giggle they can't resist.
The hour hand played hopscotch with the minute,
Squeezing time till it was in it!

Tick-tock, a dance of silly cheer,
The cogs unite, let's give a cheer!
Their laughter echoes through the night,
In a workshop where the clocks take flight.

Between the gears, they spin with glee,
Sharing secrets as they flee.
Not a soul would dare complain,
When laughter tickles like summer rain.

Glimmers of Eternity

In dreams, we find our timeless gleams,
Like treasure maps with silly themes.
A fish with wings, a cat that sings,
While clocks tick softly, play at rings.

Beyond the stars, there's a ruckus,
As time plays tricks like silly circus.
Bright gems of laughter start to fall,
Each glimmer resounds, inviting all.

A fox in slippers whirls around,
With confetti stars on playground ground.
Lost in moments, we skip and twirl,
In a timeless world, we giggle and swirl.

Through dreams we wander, hearts are bold,
Finding treasures, stories told.
Laughter echoes in the eternal stream,
Dancing through life, lost in the gleam.

The Clockmaker's Muse

In an attic where dust bunnies play,
A clockmaker hums, dreaming away.
His tools are scattered, a curious sight,
Crafting time in the pale moonlight.

With each tick, he finds his muse,
In gears and springs, he sings the blues.
A broken watch tells a tale of cheer,
Of moments lost, but still held dear.

His laughter echoes through the rooms,
As cuckoos pop with tiny booms.
"Eureka!" he shouts, and time stands still,
As clocks unite with whimsical thrill.

In the midst of chaos, a grin appears,
Ticking away all doubts and fears.
The clockmaker dreams of a grand parade,
Where time and laughter can never fade.

The Art of Fleeting Moments

In the pocket, time does dance,
Twinkling hands in a silly prance.
Ticking softly, what a tease,
Laughing hours, oh how they breeze.

Chasing shadows, we won't fret,
Giggles shared with no regret.
Every tick's a new charade,
In this circus, dreams aren't played.

Dances with Twilight

When daylight winks and shadows sway,
The seconds chuckle, come what may.
Laughter spills as dusk arrives,
Making mischief, time thrives.

Holding moments like a jest,
Napping clocks, our time's request.
Every chime a joke unwinds,
In this waltz of silly minds.

In the Company of Minutes

Minutes gather like old friends,
Joking, jostling, as time bends.
Clock hands play a game of tag,
In this fun, we dance and brag.

Silly whispers fill the air,
Time's a clown with antics rare.
Every laugh a tick we chase,
In this merry, timeless race.

Golden Gaze of Infinity

With a wink, the hours jest,
In our pockets, time takes rest.
Sunny giggles pour like gold,
While the stories laugh and fold.

Chasing dreams on a whim's flight,
Time's a jester in the night.
Every moment, a shiny prize,
In infinity's cheeky guise.

The Hour of Enchantment

Tick-tock goes the little clock,
As I search for my missing sock.
It laughs at me, a cheeky tease,
While I wrestle with my morning breeze.

The hours dance in a silly waltz,
Like my cat as it climbs the walls.
I sip my tea, then spill a bit,
And now my watch thinks I'm unfit.

Time flies by on a roller skate,
I chase it down, but it won't wait.
It giggles loud, a playful sprout,
While I loop and trip about.

Oh how the minutes make me swoon,
Like chasing shadows with a broom.
In this whimsical race we play,
I'll catch that clock—just not today!

Revelations in Every Chime

The clock strikes one, a silly sound,
With every chime, my seat's unbound.
It shakes and whirls, gives me the shake,
As I dream of pie and chocolate cake.

At two o'clock, the world's a stage,
With my watch as the antique sage.
It whispers jokes from days of old,
As I serve my tea with a side of bold.

By three, I'm lost, a giggling fool,
Debating if I should go to school.
The clock just snickers, takes a spin,
As my chaos starts to pile up within.

With every tick, my thoughts take flight,
Off to realms of pure delight.
And as the hours tick gently by,
I laugh with time—I cannot lie.

Celestial Traces

Once upon a starry night,
My wrist watch glowed, what a sight!
It tried to twirl, but lost its way,
As I made wishes in the fray.

A comet passed, it made a joke,
Telling time is just a hoax.
I chuckled back, feeling so grand,
While the universe clapped its hands.

With each tick, a giggle grew,
As cosmic dance began anew.
Planets rolled, the moon went 'whoa',
As my thoughts began to flow.

In this bizarre celestial sphere,
Every chime brought laughter near.
And in this madness, pure and bright,
Time became silly, pure delight!

Elysian Hours

In a garden where giggles bloom,
I found a clock inside a broom.
It swept away my heavy woes,
And ticked with joy, as laughter grows.

The hours played hopscotch by the sun,
Jumping high, oh what fun!
Each rhythm danced with a silly beat,
While I chased shadows on my feet.

A butterfly wore one shiny hand,
And time flew forth, just as I planned.
It fluttered wings made of sweet cheers,
As every second fell with jeers.

So here I sit in this joyful hour,
Counting giggles, feeling power.
With every tick, life's an embrace,
In this whimsical, enchanting space!

Ephemeral Journeys

In a world where time can tease,
My mind takes flight with playful ease.
Chasing seconds like a child's play,
While hours giggle and whiz away.

I wear a hat with a ticking tune,
Dancing wildly under the moon.
Each glance reveals a silly plot,
As minutes swirl, they ricochet a lot.

The sun winks, the stars twirl and dive,
In this realm, it's hard to arrive.
I chase the hours, they slip and slide,
With laughter ringing, I cannot hide.

So here's my quest, I'll spin and spin,
With time as my jester, cheeky grin.
Through laughter, I find my way back home,
In silly moments, forever I roam.

Hours Adrift Among Clouds

Up in the sky, I see a clock,
Ticking away on a fluffy rock.
I float on laughter, no reason why,
As hours parade, like birds in the sky.

Each cloud a button, I press to pause,
While time's jester bows with playful cause.
A breeze teases me with ticklish thrills,
As seconds dive off nearby hills.

Sunbeams strut in a wobbly line,
Winking at minutes, treating them fine.
While hours drift in a silly chase,
I giggle at time, in this fuzzy space.

So let's sail on this fluffy ride,
With laughter and whimsy as our guide.
For here in the clouds, so carefree and bold,
Time's secrets dance, their stories unfold.

Suspended in Elegance

A hat tipped low, a watch on a chain,
Elegance dances, but it's quite insane.
Waltzing with time, we dip and sway,
While seconds stumble in a charming ballet.

With a twirl and a giggle, I'm off my seat,
Finding mischief in each rhythmic beat.
The clock strikes a pose, dressed fancy and proud,
While laughter hides shyly beneath the cloud.

Each tick a whisper, each tock a tease,
With elegance fleeting, I sniff the breeze.
In feathered coats, the hours take flight,
Making mischief 'til the morning light.

So we'll swing and twirl, till time turns grey,
In this dance of joy, we shan't dismay.
With elegance twinkling, vie for the song,
As the world spins round, we laugh along.

The Secret Ballet of Time

In a ballroom where hours glide,
Time slips on shoes, oh so spry.
With a pirouette, the seconds prance,
While minutes giggle in flashy pants.

The walls are clocks, tickling the air,
As laughter echoes, a fancy affair.
With a wink, the stars join the spree,
In this grand show of whimsical glee.

Each tick is a tap, each tock a spin,
With backstage secrets, let the fun begin.
The clock hands jiggle, all dressed in lace,
As dusk falls softly, we keep the pace.

In this ballet of silliness, we sway,
With each joyful moment, we find our way.
Together they twirl in a timeless jest,
With a bow to the night, we revel, blessed.

The Last Tick

A tiny clock with hands that dance,
Keeps time in pants, oh what a chance!
It tickles us when it takes a break,
We start to doubt, what's real, what's fake?

The cat thinks it's a mouse in disguise,
Chasing that sound with wide-open eyes.
Each tick seems to shout, 'Woohoo!' in delight,
While we just laugh at its silly plight.

A Waltz Through Time

A waltz with hours, what a sight,
Dancing around in midday light.
Backing up seconds, never so keen,
Just one misstep, and we're lost in between.

Twirl with the minutes, let's make a bet,
Who spins the fastest? Not quite done yet!
The clock's still giggling, oh what a tease,
While we trip over time, with laughter and ease.

Daydreams of Forgotten Lanterns

In dusty corners, lanterns glow,
Lighting the thoughts that start to flow.
Their flickering, funny, makes moments twist,
A chuckle erupts, 'Did I really miss this?'

Each glow a memory, painted in hue,
They sway and chuckle, saying, 'It's true!'
With every flicker, we lose our train,
But who wouldn't, when joy is the gain?

Cartography of Moments

Maps made of laughter, oh what a plan,
Leading to places you never began.
Each corner's a giggle, each line is a jest,
Who needs a compass when you're feeling blessed?

A treasure of chuckles, a map in disguise,
With X marking spots of surprise in our eyes.
So grab hold of joy, let's wander and roam,
In this fun merry dance, we've all found a home.

Spheres of Eternal Wonder

In a world where time can dance,
Clocks wear hats and take a chance.
They giggle when the seconds tease,
And play hopscotch with careless ease.

Tick-tock, tick-tock, they sing a tune,
With every swing, they hope for June.
Time is jellied, sweet and bright,
As they paint the air with sheer delight.

A rabbit rushes, loses track,
His map of minutes feels a bit slack.
Spheres of wonder roll away,
While clocks debate the end of day.

So let's just laugh as hours float,
In silly hats, they take a boat.
We sail on giggles, fears suppressed,
As time unravels in jest, no less.

Enigmas in Every Tick

The pendulum swings with a wink of glee,
To crack the code 'tween you and me.
In each tick hides a riddle or two,
Like why socks disappear, who knew?

With every chime, they chuckle loud,
As if announcing a secret crowd.
Time's just a jester in a fancy dress,
Dancing around in playful mess.

Oftentimes, they whisper sly,
"What does it mean to let time fly?"
A waltz of whims and quirky lines,
Jokes that tick like cleverly crafted mines.

So let's embrace the playful tricks,
Find joy amidst those silly ticks.
Life's a giggle, come what may,
And clocks are just here to make us play.

Silhouettes Against the Clock

Shadows dance upon the wall,
As seconds waltz and then they fall.
In top hats, they prance with flair,
Making faces, without a care.

Each tick's a wink, a secret told,
Moments spun in glittering gold.
The sun's a hand, outstretched and bold,
Tickling dreams as they're foretold.

When midnight strikes, they all confide,
In laughter's warmth, they take a ride.
The moon giggles, while stars align,
As time plays hopscotch, oh so divine.

Join the shadows, don't miss the fun,
Life's a dance 'til the day is done.
Silhouettes laugh in a cosmic game,
While clocks tick on, never the same.

A Dance at Dusk

As daylight fades, the clocks unite,
In a dance where time takes flight.
Twisting, twirling, round and round,
They leap and giggle without a sound.

The stars peek in, with mischievous grins,
Counting seconds where the fun begins.
Each tick a step, each tock a beat,
The universe claps to the rhythm sweet.

Through colors bright, the twilight beams,
As timing's caught in silly dreams.
Time scoots around, it takes a bow,
Dressed in laughter, here and now.

So join the dance, leave worries behind,
In the dusk of wonder, serendipity's kind.
A party where giggles don't cease,
And time, it seems, likes to make peace.

Whispers of Time's Fabric

Tick-tock goes the clock, quite absurd,
It's lost in a dance, have you heard?
Hands spinning madly, oh what a sight,
Chasing their tails in the dim morning light.

A squirrel steals seconds, it makes quite a fuss,
While a cat naps away in a pocket of hush.
A waltz with the minutes, a jig with the hours,
Time giggles and wiggles, forgetting its powers.

The cuckoo is laughing, it's lost in its chime,
Making up stories, all out of time.
With each little tickle, we laughter and sigh,
As moments slip by, oh me, oh my!

So let's toast to the seconds, all silly and bright,
Spinning in circles, oh what a delight!
In the fabric of hours, let's weave a fine thread,
Of giggles and nonsense, where thoughts dance instead.

Secrets in the Quartz

Inside the old glass, secrets are spun,
With whispers of mischief and plenty of fun.
The gears start to giggle, they wiggle and bob,
Telling the tale of the old ticking mob.

A dapper old fellow, with spectacles wide,
Counts every wrinkle, no reason to hide.
But oh, the minute hand is a prankster supreme,
It picks out the moments for a whimsical dream.

Watchmakers frown, while the hands just grin,
Stealing the sunlight as it sprawls on a whim.
Inquisitive glances, oh what do they see?
A dancer with time, as time shuffles free.

So gather your laughter, let's chuckle away,
For quartz-housed secrets, we'll happily sway.
Each tick is a treasure, each tock an embrace,
In the comical realm, where time finds its place.

When Time Stands Still

There's a moment so funny, it stops in its tracks,
And all of life's hurry suddenly backs.
The clocks hold their breath, like they're startled and shy,

While seconds trade jokes, as minutes go by.

In the hush of the pause, a parade starts to play,
With elephants juggling, much to our dismay.
A dog plays the trumpet, a mouse stirs the pot,
In this whimsical calm, we've forgotten the clock!

Time kicks up its heels, and it twirls with the breeze,
As laughter erupts, like it's dancing on leaves.
In this stillness, we find an unmeasured delight,
While the hours stand still, oh what a sight!

So take off your shoes, let your spirit run free,
Embrace all the nonsense, come dance with me.
In this wacky old realm, where time spins its tale,
We'll giggle and cuddle, on a whimsical sail.

The Heirloom of Hope

In a dusty old drawer, tales linger and sigh,
Of a watch that once winked at clouds in the sky.
With hands that would fumble, and minute markers trip,
Each tick a giggle, each tock a sweet quip.

It chimes with a chuckle, a wink and a grin,
Reminding us all that it's best to dive in.
For moments like these are a treasure so rare,
When laughter inherits each tick with a flare.

The clock's a grand storyteller, oh what a delight,
It sprinkles small wishes that glimmer at night.
An heirloom of hopes, passed down through the years,
Feels heavier with laughter, lighter with cheers.

So grab hold of the whimsy, and dance through the time,
This merry old watch is a riddle and rhyme.
With giggles and dreams, let's giggle some more,
This heirloom of joy, forever we'll store.

Fantasies in a Ticking World

In a world where seconds play,
My thoughts drift far away.
A watch that giggles on my wrist,
Holds secrets too fun to resist.

Tick-tock, the silly sound,
Makes my worries spin around.
I chased a minute, slipped and fell,
It laughed so loud, 'Do you need help?'

With every chime, it jests and teases,
Counting dreams with light-hearted breezes.
Chasing time, I leap and bound,
In this merry dance, I'm joyfully drowned.

So here I am, all jumbled joy,
With a timepiece that's my favorite toy.
Each second's tick is a playful cheer,
As I twirl about, I'm free from fear.

Celestial Countdown

Stars above in a wacky race,
Count down laughter, keep your pace.
A clock that shows a silly face,
Tickles my thoughts, it's quite the chase.

While planets wobble, time fumbles too,
A quirky breeze whispers 'who knew?'
My calendar's filled with doodle trails,
Each day a story, where fun prevails.

With every hour, a dance is spun,
To a rhythm that makes you want to run.
Tickling tocks, the laughter flows,
In this cosmic joke, anything goes!

As seconds tick and laughter swells,
I'm lost in a world where all is well.
The universe winks, it knows the score,
Time's just a game, let's play some more!

Dances of Time and Light

Amidst the rays, the shadows prance,
A merry jig, a gleeful dance.
Every tick brings a funny twist,
As sunlight plays, I can't resist.

The clock, it flirts with cheeky beams,
Chasing my whims like wildest dreams.
With each glow, my laughter grows,
A ballet where time just flows.

With glassy glints that sparkle bright,
The moments shift, a fun-filled sight.
I trip and tumble in joyous flight,
As laughter echoes through the night.

So sway with me in this funny game,
Where time has no need for shame.
Together we'll twirl, jump and spin,
In a delight where we all win!

Chronicles of the Minute Hand

Once upon a ticking tale,
A minute hand rode a playful gale.
With every tick, it spun its yarn,
Gathering giggles, a source of charm.

In shenanigans, it made its rounds,
Slipping through laughter, never bound.
With stories told by a clock so wise,
Time wears a grin, a bright surprise.

Each tick and tock a quirky jest,
Filling my heart with joyous zest.
The world is a stage, and I'm the player,
Dancing with time, life's sweet betrayer.

So join the fun, embrace the flow,
Chronicles unfold, come see the show.
With every minute, let laughter arise,
In this bustling tale where joy never dies.

The Essence of Now

Ticking timepiece, what a show,
Each second flits, oh how they go.
In my pocket, trouble's bred,
A dance of time within my head.

Hurry, hurry, I race the sun,
Chasing laughs, oh what a fun!
Winding tales in a metal case,
While moments sprint at a wild pace.

Lost in thought, I misjudge the hour,
Racing thoughts like a blooming flower.
Tickle the clock, will you take a break?
I'll sip my tea, for goodness' sake!

So here's to time, in fits and starts,
With chuckles hidden in tiny parts.
A little mishap, a wink, a nod,
In this wild ride, I'll play the fraud.

Enchanted Timekeepers

In a corner, a trinket rests,
Whispering secrets of silly quests.
Each tick a giggle, each tock a jest,
Time's a jester, never at rest.

Fingers dance on a golden face,
Counting the laughs in a merry race.
What's the hour? Who needs to know?
Let's launch our dreams, let the laughter flow!

Clock hands clash like an impromptu band,
Creating rhythms both weird and grand.
My errands wait, but who really cares?
When joy is the treasure that laughter shares.

Watch them slide, the minutes gallop,
As humor blooms in a timeless wallop.
So let's be silly, let's be bright,
With chimes of mirth, we'll steal the night.

The Lullaby of the Minute Hand

A tick, a tock, as time unwinds,
In sleepy towns, a giggle binds.
The minute hand croons a soft tune,
While dreams trip lightly under the moon.

Wink at the hands as they spin about,
Whispering tales of joyous doubt.
Each tick's a tease, each tock a cheer,
As we spin tales of the silly dear.

"Don't be late!" the echoes shout,
While I'm lost in a whimsical bout.
Doodles of nonsense on every page,
Time's a clown, and we're the stage.

Come and join the watch parade,
Where time is jolly, never dismayed.
Each second a sparkle, each laugh a friend,
In this lullaby, we play pretend.

An Odyssey in Silver

Tickle the gears with a playful hand,
In silver sea, our giggles stand.
Time boats float on waves of mirth,
Navigating joy, oh what a birth!

Across the ages, we skip and slide,
With silly hats on a whimsical ride.
Jesters in time, we make our claim,
In search of laughter, we stake our fame.

A treasure hunt for the best of cheer,
With quirky maps and no real fear.
Each hour we gather more and more,
In this shiny world, who keeps score?

So here we sail, through twists and bends,
With laughter our compass, fun never ends.
In silver tides, our spirits soar,
As we dance through time, forevermore!

A Glimpse of Glimmering Dreams

In a world where time is played,
A tiny clock freaked out and swayed.
It jingled loud with every tick,
And danced around like a crazy trick.

Mice wore hats, they took the floor,
In a waltz with cheese, they begged for more.
The hands spun wild, they raced and fell,
Each backward step cast a joyful spell.

A ladybug stole the show that day,
With a spinning top that cheered her way.
They twirled beneath the candy skies,
While giggles echoed, like sweet surprise.

But all that fun, oh, what a shame,
When clocks fell down, and none felt blame.
With laughter loud, they all agreed,
Time's a prankster, indeed, indeed!

The Unfolding Second

A tiny cog began to sing,
In perfect pitch, it made us spring.
With springs that jumped and clocks that spun,
Every moment felt like pure fun.

The sun wore shades, it took a nap,
While hours danced in a silly cap.
Tick-tock races on a hill,
With goofy grins, they had their fill.

A turtle raced, oh, what a sight,
Chasing shadows with all its might.
No one could tell who'd win the game,
But laughter rang, and none felt shame.

Then suddenly, the hands froze still,
The clock was stuck, what a thrill!
With giggles loud, they tossed confetti,
For in this world, time's always petty.

Whispers Beneath the Surface

Beneath the tick-tock's jangly tune,
A fish in a suit hummed to the moon.
With bubbles popping, laughter spread,
As the second hand wiggled its head.

In tea parties held by ants on high,
With sugar cubes stacked to the sky.
They shared their stories, wild and free,
As clock hands danced with glee, oh me!

A squirrel juggled, a cheeky feat,
With acorns and nuts, such tasty treats.
The grasshoppers cheered in rhythmic hum,
A grand clock ball, oh, how they'd come!

But time, the trickster, played its game,
As minutes slipped by, none felt the same.
With a wink and a flip, they bid goodnight,
In whispers of dreams, till morning light.

Clockwork Fantasies

In a jolly realm of whirring gears,
Where laughter twirled like floating cheers.
A robot danced with a toy parade,
Twirling about in glittering shade.

Silly clocks sported daisy hats,
While kittens played on flying mats.
The wind laughed loud, it couldn't help,
While toys convened for a grand yelp.

With every tick, a new surprise,
Each second bubbled with bright blue skies.
Unicorns jumped through a rainbow's bend,
Where laughter and time danced 'round the bend.

So here's to dreams that tick away,
In a world where joy just wants to play.
Let's spin a tale full of delight,
In silly realms, we'll sing goodnight.

Timeless Whispers in Brass

In a shop where time ticks slow,
A trinket sits, its gleam aglow.
It tells tall tales from days of old,
Of watchful birds that never grow bold.

A twist of gears, a clink of glass,
As dreams collide with moments that pass.
I crack a smile at the clock's sly grin,
It winks and whispers, 'Let the fun begin!'

The Hours Between Heartbeats

A flutter here, a tick-tock there,
My heart races, caught in mid-air.
With every beat, a secret chime,
It laughs aloud at the hands of time.

Countdown to joy, what a ridiculous race,
Between each breath, there's no resting space.
I leap, I spin, a dance divine,
While seconds giggle, 'Don't lose your mind!'

Gilded Moments in the Ether

A glimmer caught beneath the bed,
A muse with mischief, just overhead.
It flutters and flaps, a golden tease,
Hints of laughter carried by a breeze.

In midst of chaos, a laugh rings clear,
Time's silly pranks bring joy near.
With every tick, my giggle swells,
As winding paths cast whimsical spells.

A Ticking Reverie

In lands where seconds frolic free,
I stumble upon a wacky spree.
A ticking friend with hands that dance,
Pulls me into a playful trance.

With every whirr, my worries fade,
Tickled by time's unending charade.
And as I twirl through swirling dreams,
I laugh and shout, 'It's not as it seems!'

A Reverie in Brass and Glass

In a world where time is a joke,
Each tick a punchline, each hand a poke.
Hats off to moments that come and go,
While laughter chimes in a bright hello.

A classic dance with gears that grin,
Counting seconds and laughs, where to begin?
With each little tick, a giggle unfurls,
As brass and glass join in silly swirls.

The dials spin stories of whimsy and cheer,
Inventing a world where clocks disappear.
Smiles in their cogs, a chuckle in brass,
In this merry realm, let the time pass!

So let's raise a toast to the silly and sweet,
To the timeless dance that never skips a beat.
In this charming jest, we find such delight,
As each second winks, in the morning light.

Timeless Whispers

Whispers of laughter, they tick away,
In corners where silliness loves to play.
Tick-tock giggles and chimes full of cheer,
Soft chuckles rumble, can you hear?

As seconds collide with mischievous glee,
A waltz of whimsy that sets us all free.
In the clock's secret, joyful hugs reside,
Where time's a prankster, the jester's guide.

Each tick tells a tale of the nonsensical kind,
Of jellybeans sprouting and trains that unwind.
So chase the quirkiness, let laughter cascade,
In the funny hushed tones that never fade.

With every turn, a riddle unfolds,
As the jokes of the universe daringly fold.
In pauses of mirth, the hours do gleam,
With timeless whispers and a wink, we dream.

Hourglass Reflections

As sand slips through in a curvy embrace,
Tickle the funny bone, give time a race.
Each grain is a giggle, each moment a jest,
In a flip of the glass, life's comedic quest.

Reflections of mischief where seconds align,
With hilarious whispers that dance out of line.
The past is a joker with stories to share,
While futures flip flops with naught but a glare.

In this comedic flow, don't count on the sand,
For laughter will tumble right out of your hand.
So pause for a punchline, a chuckle will spark,
In hourglasses spun with a wink and a lark.

Each hour they provide a new comic surprise,
A tapestry woven with fun-loving ties.
So giggle in time, let the hours unwind,
In the silly mirage where bright minds entwined.

Dreams in Ticking Hands

When hands of the clock dance a jig so spry,
Like daydreams that flutter in clear blue sky.
Each tick a tease, each tock a delight,
Plans of the silly spark laughter so bright.

Whirling and twirling, they play peek-a-boo,
With moments that bubble like fresh morning dew.
In the rhythm of time, we spin and we sway,
Chasing each tick with a grin—come what may!

Time giggles softly with mischievous charm,
Inviting us all to embrace every harm.
So rise with the laughter, let fantasies soar,
In dreams that are funny, who could ask for more?

As clocks tick with joy and pause to reflect,
Life's playful moments, we'll never reject.
So let's share the fun, let the seconds rejoice,
In a comedic symphony, let laughter be choice.

Whispers of the Gilded Hour

Tick-tock echoes from my chest,
The hands of my heart just never rest.
Each moment dances, a wiggly jig,
Sipping on laughter, a cosmic swig.

I chase the sun, but he runs so fast,
Every hour feels like a comic blast.
With every chime, I skip and prance,
In this wild world, there's no second chance.

Gilded faces with silly grins,
Counting the giggles as joy begins.
I wink at the clock, it winks back too,
Tickled by time, just me and my crew.

Moments burst like balloons of cheer,
Fun is contagious when friends are near.
So let us laugh, till the moon's aglow,
For time's a jester, putting on a show.

Fantasies on Silver Hands

Silver hands spinning in a whirl,
Painting my dreams like a raucous twirl.
I'm sailing ships made of bread and jam,
Waving at clouds, saying 'Hey, looky there!'

A clock chimes loudly at quarter past fun,
Times like these, no need for a run.
With a wink and a nod, I float right by,
In this nutty world where squirrels can fly.

Crumbs of wishes fall to the floor,
As clocks tick-tock with a rumbling roar.
I stuff my pockets with giggles galore,
In a land where silly is hardly a chore.

As I leap from 'now' to a wonderful 'then,'
With tricks up my sleeve like a crafty hen.
Life's a stage and I'm making the plans,
For the silver hands have great dance commands.

Twilight's Gentle Warning

Whispers of twilight, a comical jest,
As I trip over shadows, the day's final quest.
Rabbits in waistcoats dash to and fro,
While I juggle time like a circus show.

Mirthful chuckles spill from the sky,
What happens now? I'll just let it fly.
With stars as my audience, I twirl and spin,
In a clockwork ballet, let the fun begin!

The sun snickers softly, 'Don't lose your way,'
As mischief and magic delightfully play.
Every tick, a giggle, every tock, a smile,
Life's quirky moments make it all worthwhile.

Twilight's a trickster, never too bland,
With a wink and a nudge, it runs hand in hand.
So dance through the hours, parade through the night,
For laughter and whimsy fill the sky so bright.

Timekeepers of the Heart

Timekeepers grinning, it's quite a sight,
With faces like doughnuts, fluffy and bright.
They twiddle their thumbs, making clocks go crack,
With each silly tick, they forget to act.

Running through fields of marshmallow skies,
Where giggles grow wings and laughter flies.
A tickle, a chime, a flurry of fun,
As we play hide and seek with the ultimate sun.

Cheesy jokes echo on time's fuzzy lines,
Where whimsy reigns and joy brightly shines.
Each moment dances in a spontaneous blend,
Timekeepers of hearts, forever our friends.

So gather your dreams like butterflies rare,
And toss them in air like glittering flair.
For life's a parade, where the silly do play,
Timekeepers laughing, come join the array!

Moments Captured Between the Beats

In a pocket snug, a tiny clock,
It dances with time, a quirky mock.
Each tick a giggle, each tock a jest,
Caught in the middle, a time traveler's quest.

With hands that fumble, they chase the sun,
Whispers of laughter, oh what fun!
Minutes decay like candy floss,
In this wild ride, there's never a loss.

Winding and grinding, they shimmy and sway,
Tickling thoughts that refuse to stay.
In this tiny world, each second's a treat,
Who knew time could shuffle to such a beat?

But as the clock chuckles, we take a glance,
Forget all the worries, join the dance.
For in each second, a story unfolds,
Adventures await, oh, if time could be sold!

The Timekeeper's Reverie

With knobs and gears, a whimsical sight,
The keeper of moments, oh what delight!
He twirls his mustache, adjusts his gaze,
As time plays tricks in a playful maze.

Chasing around with a grand old grin,
He juggles the hours, let the fun begin!
Each tick a giggle, each tock a cheer,
In this quirky clockshop, we shed every fear.

Twirling through laughter, the hands they dance,
Spinning through chaos, in a whimsical trance.
Clocks chime in chorus, a raucous tune,
As time winks slyly beneath a bright moon.

Every second bubbled like soda pop,
In the land of the tickers, you'll never stop.
Laughter's the currency, freely it beams,
In the heart of the clock, we chase our dreams!

Serendipity in Stillness

In a quiet nook where the clocks take a break,
Time settles softly like a pancake.
Moments collide, each tick's a surprise,
Like finding a penny, oh what a prize!

Gears seem to giggle, their shadows have flair,
They whisper sweet nothings while time's unaware.
A glimmer of mischief twinkles in sight,
In this calm now, dreams take flight.

Lost in the charm of a curious glance,
Stillness awakens a whimsical dance.
With each gentle echo, we savor the pause,
Making time stop for our giggles and jaws.

Tickled by moments that slowly unfold,
In this curious realm, we bravely be bold.
Forget about ticking—embrace the delights,
For within this stillness, joy ignites!

Clouds of Tick-Tock

Amidst the fluff of a ticking sky,
Time floats like cotton, oh me, oh my!
Each tick a butterfly, flitting about,
As laughter escapes, there's never a drought.

Clouds shaped like clocks drift gently along,
Singing with zephyrs a joyful song.
They spin and they whirl, in a silly ballet,
Tickled by sunbeams that decide to play.

Time flies so high, we follow its lead,
Chasing the echoes of laughter and need.
In each cloud of fluff, a story takes root,
As whimsical worlds wear a tick-tock suit.

So let us float high, on whims of delight,
In the dance of the clocks, we'll take our flight.
For time is a jester, with tricks up its sleeve,
In this world of ticks, just laugh and believe!

Captured by the Quarters

In a world of dimes and nickels,
I found a tick-tock trinket,
It had me counting silly seconds,
While making snacks in the kitchen.

It giggled when I took a peek,
Teasing me with every tick,
I argued back, don't play hide-and-seek,
While invading my fridge like a little trick.

I set it down, it danced around,
A merry jig on the table found,
Pasta noodles twirled, laughter so profound,
As time became a circus, astound!

So here it spins, a jester bright,
In a world where clocks are tight,
With every chime, it brings delight,
Each quarter's joke, a silly fright.

The Pulse of Celestial Hours

In the sky's great dance, I spy,
A clock that's painted with a sigh,
Stars in a frolic, oh my oh my,
They laugh as minutes just wink by.

This cosmic watch, it wears a grin,
Planets spin in a dizzy spin,
While comets chase with a cheeky win,
Tick-tocks echo, where dreams begin.

Galaxies joke in this grand ballet,
Counting hours in their playful way,
Each twinkle says, 'Come out and play!',
As time slips past, like a cabaret.

So let's toast to this celestial spree,
A party where time is always free,
With laughter ringing, hearts filled with glee,
In the rhythm of stars, just you and me.

Tickling Dreams

In a land where the absurd reigns,
Dreams coalesce in silly chains,
Tickled pink by fluff and grains,
Time giggles along like candy canes.

Each minute's a clown on a trampoline,
Bouncing high with a zingy sheen,
Laughing as reality turns green,
A jester's hat is the new routine.

I ride on clouds shaped like pies,
Where laughter fills the sunny skies,
Each chuckle drenches all the lies,
Tickling thoughts and joyful cries.

So let's escape in this gentle breeze,
With pinches of joy, and playful ease,
With every giggle, the heart agrees,
In this tickled space where fun's the tease.

A Canvas of Time

On a canvas made of shifting hues,
Time laughs, painting its vibrant views,
With brushes of giggles and sunny clues,
It splashes joy, as life renews.

Each stroke a wink from the universe,
Conjuring laughter, avoiding a curse,
Colors of chaos, fun to immerse,
As seconds bloom in a playful verse.

Dancing clocks flutter like butterflies,
Tickled by laughter beneath the skies,
In this gallery where silliness lies,
Time's silly spirit never denies.

With every splash, the echoes tease,
In this painted world, my heart has ease,
A funny ballet on autumn leaves,
Where the canvas of time forever weaves.

www.ingramcontent.com/pod-product-compliance
Lightning Source LLC
Chambersburg PA
CBHW062108280426
43661CB00086B/343